Utopia *of the* Unicorn

THE HUNT OF THE UNICORN TAPESTRIES

A TRAVEL PHOTO ART BOOK

LAINE CUNNINGHAM

Utopia of the Unicorn

The Hunt of the Unicorn Tapestries

A Travel Photo Art Book

Published by Sun Dogs Creations
Changing the World One Book at a Time
Print ISBN: 9781946732606

Cover Design by Angel Leya

Copyright © 2018 Laine Cunningham

All rights reserved. No part of this book may be reproduced in any form or by any means, electronic, mechanical, digital, photocopying or recording, except for the inclusion in a review, without permission in writing from the publisher.

THE TRAVEL PHOTO ART SERIES

Bikes of Berlin

Necropolises of New Orleans I & II

Ruins of Rome I & II

Ancients of Assisi I & II

Panoramas of Portugal

Nuances of New York

Glimpses of Germany

Impressions of Italy

Altitudes of the Alps

Coast of California

Flourishes of France

Portraits of Paris

Knights Through the Ages

FURS AND FEATHERS

POSEY

PURE WATERS

DESIRE

FINS

HAUNTED

PEACE

STAINED

EN POINTE

BATH TIME

HIDDEN

INTO THE WOODS

ANGER

DANCE

CURLICUE

MADAM

MEEK

ALL BEAUTIFUL THINGS

CHAINED

CHECK IT OUT

FIGHT BACK

DROP SHADOW

WEEPING

CREEPING

HEALING HERBS

COLLARED

MEADOW

LAST CHANCE

MASTER OF NONE

WHO'S NEXT?

About the Author

Laine Cunningham's books take readers around the world. *The Family Made of Dust* is set in the Australian Outback, while *Reparation* is a novel of the American Great Plains. Her women's travel adventure memoir *Woman Alone: A Six-Month Journey Through the Australian Outback* appeals to fans of *Wild* and *Eat Pray Love*.

Fiction

The Family Made of Dust

Beloved

Reparation

Nonfiction

Woman Alone

On the Wallaby Track: Australian Words and Phrases

Seven Sisters: Messages from Aboriginal Australia

Writing While Female or Black or Gay

The Zen of Travel
The Zen of Gardening
Zen in the Stable
The Zen of Chocolate
The Zen of Dogs

The Wisdom of Puppies
The Wisdom of Babies
The Wisdom of Weddings

Bikes of Berlin
Necropolises of New Orleans I & II
Ruins of Rome I & II
Ancients of Assisi I & II
Panoramas of Portugal
Nuances of New York
Glimpses of Germany
Impressions of Italy
Altitudes of the Alps
Knights Through the Ages
Utopia of the Unicorn
Portraits of Paris
Flourishes of France

www.ingramcontent.com/pod-product-compliance
Lightning Source LLC
Chambersburg PA
CBHW041322110526
44591CB00021B/2875